THE SCOUT MOVEMENT IN WEST FIFE

Scouters of the 2nd Fife (YMCA) in the late 1940s. The oldest Scout Group in Fife and one of the oldest in Great Britain. Back row left to right: Jimmy Hunter; Arthur Buist; Arthur Ramage; Harry Hunter; Fred Ferguson; Sandy Jarvis; John Muir; Kenny Drysdale. Front row: Jimmy Wilson; Andrew Swan; John Foggo; Harold Hutton; Jack Castell.

THE SCOUT MOVEMENT IN WEST FIFE

Martin Rogers

TEMPUS

First published 2001
Copyright © Martin Rogers, 2001

Tempus Publishing Limited
The Mill, Brimscombe Port,
Stroud, Gloucestershire, GL5 2QG

ISBN 0 7524 2365 7

Typesetting and origination by
Tempus Publishing Limited
Printed in Great Britain by
Midway Colour Print, Wiltshire

Rosyth District Cubs at BP House 1985. Cubs from Rosyth District held a Pack Holiday at Gilwell Park in 1985 and during a trip to London they visited Baden-Powell House. Left to right in the back row are Isobel McIlroy, 68th Fife (St Peter's Parish Church Inverkeithing); Frances Stephen, 68th Fife; Margaret Glancey, 61st Fife (St John's RC Rosyth); Martin Stephen, 68th Fife; Milly Blyth, 13th Fife (Rosyth Methodist); Ian Stephen, 68th Fife; Leigh Todd; Martin Rogers, 13th Fife; and Alan Stephen, 68th Fife.

Contents

Acknowledgements

Over the last six years or so I have been involved in researching the history of the Scout Movement in the Dunfermline area as part of the Twentieth Century Dunfermline Project initiated by the Carnegie Dunfermline Trust. Much of the material I have used in this book was obtained through that project and without it this book would not have been published. My grateful thanks to the Trust for their support.

A number of people have lent me photographs either for the Carnegie Trust Project or specifically for this book and I gratefully acknowledge the assistance of:

Rod Adamson, Doug Anderson, James Brown, Derek Butchart, John Carlton, Malcolm Collens, Bill Cook, Freda Drysdale, David Dykes, Callum Farquhar, Peter Franklin, Margaret Glancey, Nigel Grey, Andy Hamilton, David Hill, Ross Kerr, Mary Kidd, Syd King, Kevin Lloyd, Elizabeth MacKenzie, Ken Marshall, Edith May, Stuart Middleton, Elaine Pert, Frank Pope, Ena Rennie, John Robertson, Drummond Sharp, Tom Simpson, Iain Smith, Phil Smithard, Lee Symms, Jim Tonner, Bert Vernolini, Dave Webster, Mary Webster, Arthur and David Welch.

I am also grateful to the following who have allowed me to reproduce photographs and other material:

Ray Allan, Lindsay Craig, Dunfermline Carnegie Library, Dunfermline Press, Earl of Elgin, Granada Studios, Morris Allan Collection at Dunfermline Carnegie Library, Norval Photographers, Scout Shops Ltd, John Shaw.

Many of the photographs have come to me from Group archives, etc. and the names of the photographers are unknown. My thanks and apologies to those photographers whose work I have not been able to acknowledge individually.

My thanks must also go to the Executive Committees of Dunfermline and Rosyth District Scout Councils for their support in the publication of this book and to The Scout Association and The Scottish Council of the Scout Association for permission to reproduce various Scout badges, postcards etc. I should make it clear that the support of these bodies does not imply any endorsement of the content of the book for which I take sole responsibility.

My Scouting history research is ongoing and I would welcome more photographs or further information about any of the photographs which appear in this book.

Martin Rogers,
161 Park Road (West),
Rosyth

Introduction

The Boy Scout Movement began in 1908 following the publication of a book 'Scouting for Boys' by Lieutenant General Robert Baden-Powell. This quickly led to Boy Scout Troops being formed in many parts of the country including Dunfermline. By the end of that year there were at least two Troops in Dunfermline – the 1st Dunfermline whose membership was drawn from boys at Dunfermline High School and the 2nd Dunfermline based on Dunfermline YMCA. The Scoutmasters were Hugh Alexander and David Allan respectively. John Foggo joined the 2nd Dunfermline the following year. In March 1909 a meeting was held to form a Local Association for the Dunfermline area and Colonel Andrew Shearer was appointed Chairman and Hugh Alexander, Secretary and Treasurer. By the beginning of 1910, three further Troops had been formed in Dunfermline. Nothing is known about the 3rd Dunfermline but the 4th Dunfermline met at the home of their Scoutmaster, Ronald Shearer, in Rose Street and the 5th Dunfermline were based at St Leonard's Church under Colour Sergeant John Ferguson. Troops had also started in Aberdour, Kelty, Cowdenbeath and Townhill.

Scouting in West Fife continued to grow and was helped by the introduction in 1914 of an experimental scheme for junior Scouts or Wolf Cubs (eight to eleven years). This too was embraced in Dunfermline and a number of Wolf Cub Packs were formed. A significant event in September 1917 was a visit to Dunfermline by Sir Robert and Lady Baden-Powell. Sadly the First World War (1914-1918) led to many Troops closing down as Scoutmasters were called to the colours. In 1919 and the 1920s, a number of new Troops and Packs were formed in Dunfermline, Inverkeithing, Aberdour, Cowdenbeath, North Queensferry, Rosyth, Kincardine, Townhill and Lassodie. Of these, two still exist today – the 41st Fife Group (initially sponsored by Rosyth Church of Scotland) and the 3rd Fife sponsored by the British Legion in Dunfermline – both of which were formed in 1925. The 1920s also saw the introduction of a number of inter-Troop competitions at District, County and National level. In 1918 a scheme for Senior Scouts was replaced with Rovers Scouts but it was not until the early to mid 1920s that Rover Crews were formed in the District. At the beginning of 1928 the new concept of Scout Groups was introduced – previously Troops and Packs had been registered separately.

The early 1930s saw an upsurge in numbers in Dunfermline District as a result of a number of new Groups being formed. In 1931 the total membership exceeded 1,000 for the first time. During the Second World War (1939-1945), a number of Scout Groups became dormant but the War did not have such a significant effect as the First World War. After the War, many Groups re-opened and by the late 1940s numbers had returned to the pre-war level. During the war there were restrictions on camping but Dunfermline

District were fortunate in being able to acquire buildings and land at Lassodie which were used as a District camp-site until 1945. In 1947 the Scottish training centre was established at Fordell Firs and this became a useful local camping facility for West Fife. By 1952 numbers in Dunfermline District had increased to over 1,500 and a separate Inverkeithing Local Association was formed comprising Groups in Rosyth, Inverkeithing and North Queensferry. In 1954 a Fife Rally was held at Raith Estate, Kirkcaldy to meet the Chief Scout, Lord Rowallan. In 1966, a new Benarty District was formed with Groups in Cowdenbeath and Kelty transferring to the new District from Dunfermline District. Also in 1966 the Advance Party Report was published leading to major changes in uniform, organisation, training programmes etc including the demise of Rover Scouts, Wolf Cubs becoming Cub Scouts, Boy Scouts becoming Scouts and the introduction of Venture Scouts. There have been further important changes since the major upheaval of the Advance Party Report. In 1976 girls were allowed to join the Scout Movement for the first time (but only in the Venture Scout section); in 1982 Beaver Scouts were introduced for six to eight-year-olds and in 1991 girls were permitted to join all sections of the Scout Movement.

In this book I have tried to record some of the important events in the history of Scouting in West Fife over the years and to illustrate some of the many activities and changes which have taken place. I am conscious that many Scout Groups which have existed in the past do not feature in this book. The same can be said of many individuals who have given long and faithful service to the Scout Movement. My appeals for photographs for the book through the Dunfermline Press and local Scout contacts met with a very limited response and in the end of the day I could only compile the book from the photographs I had. Those Groups which did provide me with photographs are better represented in the book than others but I have tried hard to include as wide a spread as possible. I hope that readers will feel that despite the gaps this book does justice to the history of the Scout Movement in West Fife.

One

Early Days

Not surprisingly there are only a few photographs in existence of the early days of Scouting in West Fife. This section, covering the first twenty years or so, brings together most of the material which has been unearthed. In West Fife we have one of the oldest Scout Groups in the country – the 2nd Fife (Dunfermline YMCA) founded in 1908 – and many of the photographs in this section come from the archives of that Group. A few (mainly poorer quality) photographs from other sources have been included to give a wider view of Scouting at that time.

Early Scouting Personalities. We begin appropriately with three key figures in the early days of Scouting in Dunfermline District. Above left is the only photograph I have been able to find of Hugh Alexander, the first Scoutmaster in Dunfermline, who led the 1st Dunfermline (High School) Troop. It is taken from the Missionary Record of 1896. Mr Alexander was an engineer and spent a number of years in the mission field at Old Calabar in Africa. He was the son of Rev. Robert Alexander of Queen Anne Street United Free Church. Above right is David Allan, the President of the Dunfermline YMCA, who started the 2nd Dunfermline Scout Troop at the YMCA and was its first Scoutmaster. He was a milliner and draper with a shop in the Maygate. He became District Commissioner in 1923 and held this position until his death in 1935. It is not known when and where this photograph of him was taken. Left is Col. Andrew Shearer, the first Chairman of Dunfermline District Local Association and one of the first District Commissioners. He is on the left of the photograph, greeting Abdalla Salama, an Egyptian Scouter visiting Dunfermline in 1922. Col. Shearer was District Chairman/President from 1909 to 1924, District Commissioner from 1914 to 1919 and an Assistant County Commissioner from 1919 to 1934. When he finally gave up active Scouting he was over eighty years old.

Scout Rally 1910. This is the earliest known photograph of Scouting in this area. It is of the first Public Rally held in the Public Park, Dunfermline on 30 April 1910. About 3,000 spectators watched the demonstrations put on by six Scout Troops (including one from Cowdenbeath) and a Troop of Girl Guides. The two men on the left are Col. Shearer (District Chairman) and Lieut. Moubray RNVR, Commissioner for West Fife. In the centre by the bell tent is the inspecting officer, Col. Hunt, and Ronald Shearer, Scoutmaster of the 4th Dunfermline Troop and also local adjutant. Amongst the group of Scouts to the right of Lieut. Moubray is Ronald Stevenson who later became Chairman of the District (1952-1965). (Photo by James Kirkhope)

2nd Fife c.1911. A group of 2nd Fife Scouts on an outing (probably from camp). Scoutmaster David Allan is on the right of the photograph. (Dunfermline Carnegie Library – Local History Collection)

2nd Fife *c.*1911. Another group of 2nd Fife Scouts in camp at flag break probably at Nineacres. On the right is Scoutmaster John Foggo. (Dunfermline Carnegie Library – Local History Collection)

Charlestown Scouts *c.*1911. Lord Bruce was an active supporter of the local Charlestown Scout Troop. A Press report of 1911 refers to Lord Bruce training them in farming operations and driving them to and from their work in his motor. Could this be what is happening here? The car is an Argyll. Lord Bruce is in the driving seat with William Black, manager of the Limeworks, immediately behind him.

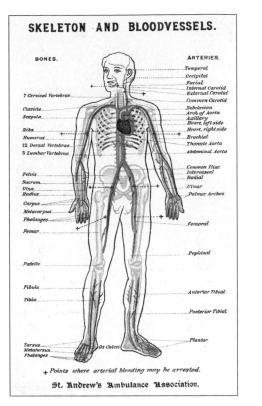

Above left – Ambulance Class Handout 1911. A local GP, Dr William Barrie Dow, ran ambulance classes for the Scouts and Boys' Brigade and produced this handout for those taking part. On the reverse side is a diagram showing the skeleton and blood vessels. Above right and below – 2nd Fife in camp 1912. Fortunately these two photographs are dated. They show two popular Scouting activities – bathing and eating. This site at Crook of Devon (Nineacres) was used by the Troop from its early days. Scoutmaster David Allan appears in both photographs. (Dunfermline Carnegie Library – Local History Collection)

13

Scouts 1912. Apart from a date on the drum there is no other information about this photograph. It is tempting to suppose that this is the 2nd Fife once again but the neckerchief appears to be two-coloured and neither of the two well-known Scouters of the 2nd Fife are in the photograph. (Dunfermline Carnegie Library – Local History Collection)

Scouts in Camp c.1912. This is almost certainly the 2nd Fife at their camping site at Nineacres. (Dunfermline Carnegie Library – Local History Collection).

Rosyth Navvy Mission Troop 1916. The first Scout Troop in Rosyth was formed in 1915 by Mr Darwin Needham, the Village Missionary. The Troop were successful in the first inter-Troop competition for a silver bugle 'The Gibb Bugle' and they are pictured here with the bugle in 1916. The adults are Assistant Scoutmaster C.P. Hoff, Scoutmaster Needham and Petty Officer Roberts. The Gibb Bugle is still competed for annually by troops in Dunfermline District. (Photo by Norval).

Rosyth St Margaret's Cubs and Scouts c.1920. A Scout Troop and Cub Pack were formed at St Margaret's Anglican Church and they met in Douglas Block – one of the buildings on Castle Road. In the original photograph their name is just visible on the flag. Stanley Elmes was the Scoutmaster and Cubmaster and he could well be the man at the right of the back row.

Rosyth Cubs and Scouts *c.1920*. There is no information about this photograph other than the Troop was from Rosyth.

Victoria Scouts Football Team *c.1920*. A Scout Troop known as the 17th Fife (Victoria) Troop was formed in 1917 and met in Viewfield Baptist Church. Their Scoutmaster was William Sharp and his son (also William) is fourth from the left in the back row. He was an Assistant Scoutmaster and was later Scoutmaster of the 26th Fife (Viewfield Baptist) and Group Scoutmaster of the 13th Fife (Rosyth Methodist) Groups. (See photograph at the top of p.36).

Demonstration of Scouting 1923. Rev. W.N. Gordon Boxer was the Scoutmaster of the 43rd Fife (St Andrew and St George Episcopal Church Rosyth) and involved the Scouts in performing sketches and plays. They were staged at various venues but their top billing must have been in this production at the Opera House. This was a District event involving also the 2nd Fife (YMCA) orchestra and an entertainment by the 1st Fife (Dunfermline High School) Pack. During the performance, the 43rd Fife were presented with the Gibb Bugle which they had won that year – the first time the competition had been held since 1916.

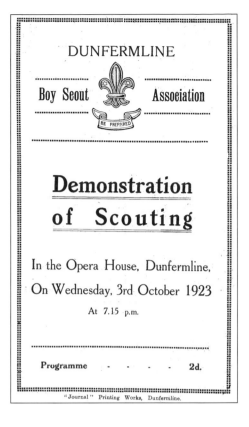

DUNFERMLINE

Boy Scout Association

BE PREPARED

Demonstration

of Scouting

In the Opera House, Dunfermline,
On Wednesday, 3rd October 1923

At 7.15 p.m.

Programme - - - - 2d.

"Journal" Printing Works, Dunfermline.

This studio photograph is of Bob Marshall, a member of the 17th Fife (Crombie) Troop c.1924. The badge above his pocket is presumably the Tenderfoot and on his left arm is what appears to be a Second Class Badge. (Photo by J. & A. Fowlis).

2nd Fife Contingent for the Imperial Jamboree 1924. In 1924, an Imperial Jamboree was held in Wembley Stadium attended by about twenty-four Scouts and Scouters from West Fife. The Jamboree was either part of or ran side by side with an Imperial Exhibition in London. This is the contingent from the 2nd Fife (YMCA) left to right, back row: Scout J. Buist; SPL R. White; PL Alex Robertson; SPL P. Hume; SPL W Nicoll. Front row: PL Gow, Assistant Scoutmaster Duncan Ritchie; Scoutmaster John Foggo; PL D. Morwood; PL Aitken. (Photo by Norval).

2nd Fife Scouts, mid 1920s. The 2nd Fife Scouts about to set off for camp from their headquarters (the YMCA premises in Damside Street) which was a regular venue for District meetings. When the building was taken down, part of it was taken to Nineacres and became the Cub hut there.

3rd Fife Scouts in Camp *c.*1927. The 3rd Fife (British Legion) were founded in 1925 and had their first few summer camps on the Tulliallan Estate, Kincardine on Forth. Perhaps that is where this photograph was taken. The Scouter is probably the first Scoutmaster William Wilkie. In the foreground is Dr Alan Tuke, a member of the British Legion and a supporter of the Scout Movement. He later became President of Fife County Scout Council and was invested as a Rover Scout at the age of about seventy.

34th Fife, Holy Trinity, in Camp *c.*1927. A Scout Troop was started at the Holy Trinity Church, Dunfermline, in 1925 with Willie Alexander as the first Scoutmaster. These Scouts from the Troop were in camp with the British Legion Troop.

Above left – 3rd Fife Scouts *c.*1927. Another photograph of 3rd Fife Scouts – this time the Patrol Leaders and Seconds. The lady in the middle is probably the Cubmaster Eva Templeman who was a Scouter and Assistant District Commissioner for many years and also served as District Treasurer during the Second World War. Above right – Wedding of Charles Cook and Charlotte Fernie 1928. Scout weddings with guards of honour are not uncommon but it is unusual for the groom to wear Scout uniform for the occasion! Scoutmaster Charles Cook and Lady Cubmaster Charlotte Fernie both of the 44th Fife (St Leonard's) Group were married on 7 September 1928. Below – 2nd Fife in Camp *c.*late 1920s. The 2nd Fife (YMCA) have traditionally held a Group camp and here we see Cubs, Scouts and Rovers gathered for a camp photograph probably in the late 1920s. Amongst those who can be identified are David Allan on the extreme left, John Foggo on the extreme right and Duncan Ritchie in front of the door of the bell tent towards the right of centre.

Two
Wolf Cubs and Rover Scouts

Young boys were soon clamouring to be Scouts and some unofficial Junior Scout Troops were being formed. Baden-Powell decided to put this on a proper footing and in January 1914 launched an experimental scheme for Junior Scouts or Wolf Cubs. This took Rudyard Kipling's *The Jungle Book* as its background. Dunfermline District were quick to take up this new development and by the end of the year there were Packs associated with the 2nd Dunfermline (YMCA) and Charlestown Troops and possibly others. The scheme proved very successful and the Wolf Cub section was formally inaugurated into the Scout Movement in December 1916 with the publication of the *Wolf Cub's Handbook*. Photographs of Wolf Cubs are included in this section of the book up to 1967 when the Wolf Cubs changed their name to Cub Scouts.

A scheme for older boys (Senior Scouts) was introduced in May 1917 and in August 1918 they were re-named Rover Scouts. The handbook *Rovering to Success* was published in June 1922. Rover Crews were formed at the 27th Fife (St Margaret's Anglican Church Rosyth) in 1922, the 2nd Fife (YMCA) in 1925 and at the 3rd Fife (British Legion) and 19th Fife (Queen Anne School) in 1927. Other Groups formed Crews at various times but it often proved difficult to sustain these over long periods of time. Regular Rover gatherings (Moots) were held at County, National and International level. Rover Scouts ceased to exist when the new Venture Scout section was introduced in 1967.

Rosyth Wolf Cubs c.1922. Little is known about this group of Wolf Cubs other than they were from Rosyth. The Red Triangle Club in Rosyth (part of the YMCA) had started a Cub Pack in 1918 and perhaps this was that Pack.

2nd Fife Cubs mid 1920s. This is probably a group of 2nd Fife (YMCA) Cubs taken at Nineacres. It was among photographs belonging to Abe Johnston. Neckerchiefs were worn loosely knotted at the neck until about 1924 when woggles were introduced. As the Cubs here are wearing woggles the photograph would have been taken after that date.

2nd Fife Cubs late 1920s. Another group of 2nd Fife (YMCA) Cubs with leaders Duncan Ritchie on the left and Alex Robertson on the right.

3rd Fife Cubs 1931. The 3rd Fife (British Legion) Cubs in Abbey Park Place outside the old squash court which was their meeting place. The adults in the back row are thought to be Assistant Cubmaster Jenny Carmichael; Assistant District Commissioner Duncan Ritchie; Cubmaster Eva Templeman; a gentleman from India studying at Dunfermline College of Physical Education and a Miss Miller.

Lady Cubmasters early 1930s. On the left is Mrs Florence Clouston, Cubmaster of the 41st Fife Rosyth; in the middle is Mary Amos formerly of the 41st Fife but by then Cubmaster of the 57th Fife (United Free Abbey Church) based at Rumblingwell Mission; and on the right, Jean Moncrieff of the 52nd Fife (Rosyth Baptist).

57th Fife Cubs in camp early 1930s. Cubs from the 57th Fife (United Free Abbey) Pack in camp at Tapitlaw Farm, Comrie. Two of the three ladies are Alice and Nettie Reid, daughters of the minister of the Church, and the third is a Miss Yuill, daughter of the farmer. The Cub Pack had won the inaugural District Cub football league competition in 1931 and perhaps this photograph was taken to mark the occasion.

61st Cubs in Camp late 1930s. Kit inspection at camp for these Cubs of the 61st Fife (St John's RC Church Rosyth).

2nd Fife Cubs meeting 'Oliver Twist' 1949. John Howard Davis who played Oliver Twist in the film of that name visited Dunfermline in March 1949. He took part in a quiz at the Palace Kinema with this group of Cubs from the 2nd Fife (YMCA). They are, left to right – Derek Hutton (partly hidden); Frank Malcolm; Bert Vernolini; Sandy Christie; Bobby Jarvis; Ewan Johnston and Billy Hendry.

44th Fife Cubs' Outing mid 1950s. A group of Cubs from the 44th Fife (St Leonard's) on an outing. Amongst the adults in the back row are May Adamson, Bob Clough (fourth from right), Alex Adamson (third from right) and Stuart Sayer (on right).

96th Fife Cubs' Outing 1961. Cubs from the 96th Fife (Canmore Congregational Church) on an outing – probably at Edinburgh Zoo. The Scouter is Ethel Welch. Although green jerseys are associated with Cubs, it was permissible for Packs to wear navy blue, khaki or grey jerseys. Here the 96th Fife are wearing grey jerseys.

41st Fife Cubs 1966. In 1966 the Wolf Cubs celebrated their golden jubilee and Packs were encouraged to have a Pack photograph taken. The 41st Fife (Rosyth) Pack are seen here with their Cubmaster John Lyson.

13th Fife (Rosyth Methodist) Cubs 1966. Another jubilee photograph. Left to right back row: Finlay MacConnachie; Ian Woodhead; Robert McKelvie; Gordon Hood; John Smith; Donald Whiting; Keith Pascoe. Second back row: Neil Pearson; James Hood; Ian Paterson; Clive Allan; Martin Laurenson; Douglas Swatton; George Varney. Leaders: Trevor Hayes; Martin Rogers; Mary Murray; Tom Pearson; Stuart Fowell. Front row Stephen Lawson; David Laurenson; James Stewart; Derek Lomass; Mark Payne; Kenneth Jappy; Bobby Read.(Photo by Ray Allan)

2nd Fife Rovers 1926. A group of Rovers in camp at Nineacres. Left to right back row: D. Scott; J. Lister; John Downie; Jim Buchanan. Middle row: J. Muir; A. Shepherd. Front row: A. Robertson; Bill Anderson; Don Simpson. John Foggo is in the background.

19th Fife Rovers, early 1930s. There was a strong Rover Crew in the 19th Fife (Queen Anne Junior Secondary School). In this portion of a photograph we have left to right, back row: Stewart Hepburn; Donald Mackay (Rover Scout Leader and English Teacher); David Lugton (Scoutmaster and Asst English Teacher); Reg Lang. Front row: Sandy Young; Tom Chrystal; Hugh Cumming and George Lister.

2nd Fife Rovers, *c.*1930. During their summer camp at Nineacres the 2nd Fife (YMCA) used to organise a concert and dance in Fossoway Village Institute with the proceeds being shared between the Nursing Association and Institute Fund. Above – a group of 2nd Fife Rovers after the dance in about 1930. Left to right, back row: J. Buist; J. Wilson; Harry Forrest; P. Hume; B. Jarvis; J. Muir. Second back row J. Smith; and Tom Duncan. Front row: J. Stoddart; Tom Ramage and George Aitken. In the very front is Andrew Swan. Below – some of the Rovers dressed for their parts in the concert (date unknown).

43rd Fife Rovers, 1932. These Rovers were attached to the 43rd Fife (St Andrew and St George Episcopal Church Rosyth) and were on an outing to Aberdour in June 1932.

2nd Fife Hut at Cults Hill, 1937. The 2nd Fife (YMCA) Crew had a hut on Cults Hill, Saline which was the setting for their annual Christmas dinner. This is a group of Rovers from the 2nd Fife and 19th Fife (Queen Anne School) at the hut in the summer months of 1937.

Fife Rover Moot 1938. Fife Rovers held an annual moot and in 1938 this was held at Broomhead Park, Dunfermline. In this group are the Rev. Robert Dollar (Dunfermline Abbey); John Foggo, 2nd Fife (YMCA); Dr Alan Tuke; Major John Lumsden (County Commissioner) and Lord Glentanar (Chief Commissioner for Scotland). At the Moot, Major Lumsden was presented with the Silver Wolf. (Photo by Dunfermline Journal).

2nd Fife Rovers 1944. Another group of 2nd Fife (YMCA) Rovers taken at camp. Left to right, back row: A. Rattray; J. Nisbet; J. Duncan; D. Caldwell; J Thompson. Middle row: G. Cree; J. Wilson; Fred Ferguson; G. Storie; D. Sinclair. In front: S. Paterson and A. Petrie.

Fife Rover Moot *c.*1949. There is no indication of when and where this photograph was taken. It appears to be a gathering of Rover Scouts and may well have been the Fife Rover Moot held at Cowdenbeath in May 1949. Those identified are Kenny Drysdale 2nd Fife (YMCA) at the left end of the back row; in the second front row are left to right David Benzie, Frankie Miller and Tommy Sime – all 41st Fife (Rosyth), Jimmy Scotland and Archie McEwan – both 2nd Fife; Davie Rodger, 46th Fife (Cowdenbeath YMCA); -?-; Dougie Watson and Frank Bell (?) – both 2nd Fife; Jimmy Spence, 41st Fife and Sandy Cree, 2nd Fife . In the middle of the group of three seated in the front left of the photo is George Munro of the 77th Fife (Kelty Oakfield).

2nd Fife Rover Investiture, *c.*1951. A Rover investiture was an important and solemn occasion and included the ritual of washing of hands. This investiture took place during the annual camp of the 2nd Fife (YMCA) at Nineacres. Left to right Tom Simpson (with flag), Marcus Johnston (with jug), Ronnie Laing, Tom Foggo, Jimmy Duncan, Sandy Johnstone, David Birrell.

2nd Fife Rovers at Camp, 1952. A more formal group of 2nd Fife (YMCA) Rovers and Officers in camp. Left to right, back row: Rev. Hugh Henderson; Marcus Johnston; George Storrie; Ronnie Laing; Jim McEwan; 'Doc' Jack Gilmour. Second back row: Dave Watson; Davie Birrell; Frank Bell; David Scott; Arthur Henderson; Hamish Mathieson; Sandy Johnstone; Tom Grant. Second front row: Archie McEwan (with flag); Jack Castell; Andrew Swan; Harold Hutton; Simon Hunter (behind); Rev. J. Brackenridge; Tom Foggo; Tom Simpson (with flag). Seated at front: Charlie Mathieson; Martin McGoram; Tony Harris.

3rd Fife Rovers c.1954. Four members of the 3rd Fife (British Legion) Rover Crew at a Fife Rover Moot at Nineacres in January. Left to right: Ed Mapstone; Peter Franklin; Fred Lingwood and Willie Robertson.

2nd Fife Rovers with Sir Compton Mackenzie, 1959. Some of the 2nd Fife (YMCA) Rovers being introduced to Sir Compton Mackenzie, who was in Dunfermline in connection with the screening of the film 'Rockets Galore'. Left to right – D. Grieve; Bert Vernolini; M. Scott; S. Steele; H. McLean; I. McIntosh; George Baillie; J. Ritchie; R. Donn; Tony Harris; T. Grant. (Photo by Peter Leslie).

Scottish Rover Moot, 1967. County Commissioner, Capt. David Fairlie, and Admiral Superintendent, Rear Admiral Ridley, with some of the 2nd Fife Rover Scouts at the last Scottish Rover Moot to be held (at Fordell Firs). Left to right back row: Tony Harris; Sandy Callum; Jock Baillie; David -?-; Gordon Penrose. Front Row: Garry Whinnie; Marcus Simpson and Stuart Macpherson. (Photo by Dunfermline Press).

Three
Fordell Firs

In 1947, Scottish Headquarters established a Training Centre at Fordell Firs. This was later made available for Scout camping. Although Fordell Firs is a national centre, Scouting in West Fife has always been closely associated with it. Abe Johnston, then DC for Dunfermline District, was involved with the development of the site and local Rovers gave practical help. The 87th Fife Rover Crew at HMS Caledonia were particularly involved and were given the use of a cottage at the Hillend Road entrance as a base. They named it AFIA (Away From It All). Over the years, many of the Wardens and support staff have been drawn from Dunfermline and Rosyth Districts. The Centre has been changed and developed in recent years and is now also the home of Scottish Headquarters which moved from Edinburgh in 1987.

Wood Badge Course 1947. The 76th Scottish Wood Badge Course (but the first to be held at Fordell Firs) includes two known faces – John Lyson (then a Scouter with an Edinburgh Sea Scout Troop) and William Sharp, 13th Fife (Rosyth Methodist). Only the surnames of the participants are given and they are, left to right, back row: Johnston; Wang; Rhind; Lyson. Middle row: Barrie; Chirnside; Munro; Hendrie; Faishney; Basham; Bell; McDonald. Front row: -?-; James Barrie, Fife County Secretary and ACC (Training); Alex Lawson, Field Commissioner; John 'Denny' Henderson, Field Commissioner; L. Smith; Jamieson; Sharp; Belford. The participants were formed into patrols for the course hence the temporary Patrol Leaders and Second stripes being worn by some of the members.

The Headquarters Hut c.mid 1950s. This was sited near the Richmond Chalet. It was demolished within about the last ten years.

The Flagpole *c*.mid 1950s. A view of the flagpole from the entrance to the chapel with the totem on the right.

The Training Field *c*.mid 1950s. The training field is the area behind the present day Scottish Headquarters building. There were four patrol/six sites (with huts) which were used during wood badge training courses. This was the site used either by the Grey Six or Otter Patrol depending on whether it was a Cub or Scout training course. Behind the site is the area now used for the assault course.

Opening of the Richmond Chalet 1955. The Richmond Chalet is named after Sir John Richmond of Ayrshire who provided the money to build it. Much of the work was done by voluntary labour and the final bill for its construction was less than £1,000. This is the official opening of the Chalet on 4 September 1955. Dunfermline's District Commissioner Abe Johnston is fourth from the left.

Dodds Hut and David Reid Lounge 1975. The Dodds Hut on the left (named after a former Scottish Headquarters Commissioner for Cubs) and the Jubilee Hut behind were badly damaged by fire on 13 May 1984 and had to be demolished. The David Reid lounge on the right continued in use until it was demolished to make way for the new All Weather Activity Centre opened in 1997.

Rosyth District Scout Camp 1979. During the camp, Cubs and Scouts from Rosyth District planted a group of trees (most of which have still survived!). Below District Commissioner John Lyson organises things while warden Norman Maudsley and his wife Pat look on.

Rosyth District Cubs Go Kart Rally 1979. For a few years, Rosyth District Cubs held a go-kart rally in the Boys' Field at Fordell. Amongst the leaders at the back are – on the left: John Sherwood, 49th Fife (Rosyth). In the centre: Vic Fox, 13th Fife (Rosyth Methodist); Margaret Glancey, 61st Fife (St John's RC Rosyth) and Linda Sherwood, 49th Fife. On the right: Maureen Pyke, 48th Fife (Dalgety Bay).

Rosyth District Cub Camp 1981. Cubs from various Rosyth District Packs assemble in the open air chapel for a Cubs' Own. The leaders at left of centre are Bob Todd and Ken Cooper (with the woolly hats) of the 41st Fife (Rosyth) and Jerry Pyke of the 48th Fife (Dalgety Bay). In front of Ken are Frances and Ian Stephen of 68th Fife (St Peter's Parish Church Inverkeithing). The leaders on the right are from the 49th Fife (Rosyth).

Scottish Headquarters Building 1986. The new building for Scottish Headquarters taking shape in August 1986.

Four

In the Public Eye

Scouting activities are generally carried out away from the public gaze – in Scout headquarters, in the countryside and at camp or pack holidays. However, there are occasions when the activities are deliberately aimed at attracting or involving the public e.g. for publicity and recruitment reasons, good turns and fund raising. The first such event was in Dunfermline Public Park in 1910 (see page 11) and another was the demonstration in the Opera House in 1923 (see page 17). The photographs in this section look at some of these activities over the years.

Please Pass on this Information to your Assistant Scouters.

THE BOY SCOUTS ASSOCIATION
THE SCOTTISH HEADQUARTERS . . .
TELEGRAMS: . . . "FRATERNITY, EDINBURGH."
TELEPHONE 27435

44 CHARLOTTE SQUARE,
EDINBURGH, 1ST MAY 1931.

ANNUAL CONFERENCE
OF THE
SCOTTISH HEADQUARTERS COUNCIL
6th and 7th June 1931

DEAR SCOUTER,

I have the pleasure of intimating the arrangements for this year's Conference, and, on behalf of the Conference Sub-Committee, giving you a hearty invitation to join us there. After the success which attended the Conference at Stirling last year, a record attendance is expected at Dunfermline, and I would urge you to do your best to help towards that end. The programme will convince you that it will be well worth while.

The Conference sessions will be held in the Unitas Halls in Queen Anne Street, a most comfortable suite of rooms, situated in close proximity to the billets and catering hall.

Accommodation.—Through the kindness of the Carnegie Dunfermline Trust, billets will be available in the Pilmuir Hall, and for those who prefer the open air, a convenient camping site is offered at the Trust's Sport Ground at Venturefair.

The Lady Cubmasters will be accommodated in the comfortable club premises in Abbey Park Place, kindly offered by Mrs. Bishop.

Blankets and Matresses will be provided, but it is advisable to bring a rug or extra blanket with you.

Those who desire hotel accommodation are requested to make their own arrangements. The following hotels are recommended :—The Royal Hotel, High Street, and Fraser's Hotel, Bridge Street. The Headquarters Officials (London and Edinburgh) will be at the former.

Guides will meet the principal train and bus arrivals, and conduct members to billets and camp.

Catering.—All meals will be served in the Dunfermline Co-operative Society's Hall in Randolph Street (across the street from the Unitas Halls) and a generous menu has been arranged for. This year it will be possible to supply odd meals, **provided these are ordered beforehand,** as detailed on the Registration Form attached. Many appreciations of the value of feeding together were received after last year's Conference, and it is hoped that this will be fully taken advantage of. Members staying in hotels are asked to take all meals, other than breakfast, at the hall.

Arrangements are being made for facilities for cooking at the camp for those who wish to undertake their own catering.

Cost.—This year a Registration Fee of 1/- per member will be charged. Feeding for the whole period, 9/-. Use of blankets and mattress, 1/6.

Scottish Conference in Dunfermline 1931. In 1931 (and again in 1950) Dunfermline hosted the annual Scottish Conference. This is the front page of the circular letter issued by Scottish Headquarters about the arrangements. Thrift was very much in evidence with participants being given the opportunity to camp or sleep on the floor of the Pilmuir Hall. Although not a public event as such, the presence of so many Scout uniforms in Dunfermline must have raised the Scouting profile.

Scout Rally East End Park 1934. The finale
to a Scout Week held in Dunfermline in June
1934 was a Rally and demonstration at East
End Park. On the right is the programme
cover and below are the Cubs preparing for a
grand howl.

Jubilee Bonfires 1935. When celebration bonfires were required the Scouts were usually asked to build them. Here we see two bonfires prepared for the Silver Jubilee of King George V in May 1935. The one on the left was on the Whinny Hills at North Queensferry and was built by Scouts from Rosyth and Inverkeithing. The leader at the bottom is Harold Jackson of the 61st Fife (St John's RC Church Rosyth). At the very top are leaders from the 52nd Fife (Rosyth Red Triangle) left to right: John Wallace; Jimmy Patterson; Andy Wilson and Jean Moncrieff. Below is a bonfire built by Cowdenbeath Rover Scouts on Hill of Beath.

2nd Fife Rovers in Hospital Pageant *c.*1939. The 2nd Fife (YMCA) Rovers took part regularly in the annual pageants to raise funds for the hospital. They are pictured here dressed for the occasion outside their hall in Damside Street.

2nd Fife Rovers in Hospital Pageant *c.*1949. On the lorry are left to right Archie McEwan, Frank Bell, Murray Cumming, Marcus Johnston, Tom Paton and Tom Foggo. David Watson is the one seated, Gavin Mann wears the L plate and Ronnie Wilson is standing beside the lorry.

2nd Fife Gang Show 1949. Gang Shows became a popular way of raising funds and the ones put on by the 2nd Fife were very polished shows staged at the Carnegie Hall and playing to packed houses. This is the cast of the 1949 Gang Show and the three Scouters in the middle of the third front row are Scoutmaster Andrew Swan; Group Scoutmaster John Foggo and Scoutmaster Harold Hutton. There is a certain poignancy to this photograph as John Foggo died suddenly on the opening night of the Show. (Dunfermline Press).

Youth Parade 1949. Dunfermline Civic Weeks began in 1948 and incorporated a Youth Parade to Dunfermline Abbey. Here the colours of Dunfermline District are carried into the Abbey by Jimmy Lawson and Roy Whiting of the 13th Fife (Rosyth Methodist) who had won the Gibb Bugle that year. Providing a guard of honour are Ian Allardyce; Mike Gill and Billy Gow of the 41st Fife (Rosyth). The Scouters behind are Harold Hutton, 2nd Fife (YMCA); Andy Wilson (Assistant District Commissioner) and William Sharp (13th Fife). (Photo by West Fife Photos).

41st Fife Tableau 1952. The cast of a tableau entered in Rosyth Gala by the 41st Fife (Rosyth) Cubs obviously on a Pirates theme.

Youth Parade c.mid 1950s. Scouts in the annual Youth Parade make their way down Kirkgate to the Abbey. The contingent from the 44th Fife (St Leonard's) are in the middle of the photograph. Left to right the colour party is Bruce Thomson; Harry Hamilton and Roy Hunter. The two leaders behind are Bob Clough and Jim Reekie. (Photo by Morris Allan).

81st Fife Gang Show 1958. The 81st Fife (1st Broomhall) put on a Gang Show in the Queen's Hall, Charlestown, on two nights in February 1958. They were assisted by Rover Scouts from the 87th Fife (HMS Caledonia) Rover Crew.

Inverkeithing District Parade 1960. An unusual view of a St George's Day Parade taken inside the Methodist Church in Rosyth. The minister (and Cubmaster) of the Church, Rev. Robert Collens, is leading the service with James Scott (District Chairman) to the left and Jimmy Spence (41st Fife) and Assistant District Commissioner John Prior to the right.

Youth Parade *c.*1964. The contingent from the 39th Fife (St Margaret's) make their way down Kirkgate with Troop Leader John Philp carrying the flag. Behind him are David Lawson; Scouter Ken Marshall; Jimmy Roxburgh; Billy Manclark and Russell Mann. To the left of John Philp are Jimmy Lawson and Alistair Beck. (Photo by Peter Leslie).

Youth Parade 1965. In this contingent of Cubs from Inverkeithing District led by John Lyson are members of the 67th Fife (North Queensferry), 41st Fife (Rosyth), 52nd Fife (Rosyth Baptist) and 49th Fife (St Andrew and St George Rosyth). Amongst the leaders bringing up the rear is Sarah Giles (67th Fife). The Cub in front of John Lyson is from the 104th Fife (Holy Trinity). (Photo by Peter Leslie).

Rally in Glen 1965. A Rally was held in the Glen in June to welcome the Chief Commissioner for Scotland, the Captain of Dunstaffnage. He is seen here with (left to right) Eddie Thomson, ADC (Cubs) for Dunfermline; Abe Johnston, County Commissioner and John Prior, DC for Inverkeithing District.

Rally in Glen 1965. The Cubs perform a Grand Howl at the opening of the Rally with the 13th Fife (Rosyth Methodist) nearest the camera. (Photo by Ray Allan)

2nd Fife Cubs 1965. Cubs from the 2nd Fife (YMCA) at the rally in the Glen in 1965. Left to right, back row: Robert Moyes, Tom Simpson, Graham Brotherston. Cubs standing include Alan Jamieson (second from left); Gavin Erskine (fourth from left); Sandy Hudson (sixth from left); Billy Best (fifth from right); George Black (fourth from right); Ross Hamilton (?) (on right). On the left in the middle row is Alistair Justice with Malcolm Bruce third from the left. In the second front row is Billy McEwan (second from right) and David Shand (on right). In the front row is Tommy Gray (third from left) and Hamish Donaldson (fourth from left).

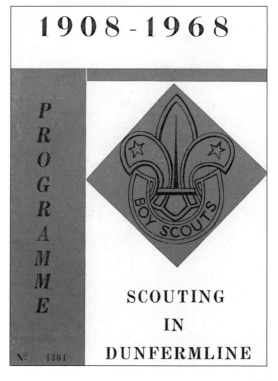

Diamond Jubilee Celebrations 1968. As part of their diamond jubilee celebrations, Dunfermline District held a Jamborette in Pitreavie Playing Fields on 22 June 1968. This is the cover of the souvenir programme.

1908 - 1968

PROGRAMME

SCOUTING IN DUNFERMLINE

Civic Week Parade of Floats early 1970s. The float entered by the 40th Fife (Touch) in the Civic Week Parade. The date is not known but going by the banner would probably be in the early 1970s. In the canoe is Alan Lawson with Craig Innes beside him. The Scouter is Ian Parnell. (Photo by Morris Allan).

Rosyth District Open Days 1971. In the early 1970s, Rosyth District staged a number of open days in Rosyth Public Park. The aerial runway proved a popular attraction. Stephen Lucas of the 13th Fife (Rosyth Methodist) is about to set off.

A special part of the Scout Job Week, 1972, was a shoe shine and here Scouts from the 39th Fife (St Margaret's) are touting for business outside their Church in East Port. Having their shoes shone are left to right: Mr Meldrum, John Philp and Willie Goodwin. The two Scouts on the left are Derek Meldrum and Barry Hailstones and on the right are Billy Bower, David Anderson, David Jolly, Chris Fielding and Craig Seath with Ross Marshall behind. (Dunfermline Press).

Clean Up 1981. The 39th Fife (St Margaret's) became clean up champions (see page 74). They are pictured here with some of the rubbish they collected. In the left foreground are Andrew Spowart and Alastair Barclay. Standing on top are left to right Barry Hailstones, Lindsay Short and Douglas Hamilton. Crouching are Paul Mitchell and Michael Kirk and in the right foreground are Euan Robertson and Graham Young.

Beach Clean Up 1986. A squad from the 81st Fife (1st Broomhall) who took part in a beach clean up at Limekilns. Left to right, at the back are Craig Mitchell; Alan Milligan; Alan Helmore; -?-; -?-; -?-; Calum Mitchell and Ian Lucas. In front are Elizabeth MacKenzie; Michael Hambley; -?-; ? Ragg and Jimmy Hutchison.

Rosyth District Parade 1994. The Parade leaves Rosyth Methodist Church after their annual St George's Day Service. Kevin Lloyd of the 68th Fife (St Peter's Parish Church Inverkeithing) is on the extreme left and Paul Ward of the 13th Fife (Rosyth Methodist) is nearest the camera holding the Union Flag. Jean Shaw of the 13th Fife leads the procession with one of her Beavers, Alasdair West. Behind her is Elaine Pert of the 48th Fife (Dalgety Bay) with Beaver Gareth Coster followed by Alan Thomson and Frank Crozier of the 41st Fife (Rosyth).

Five

Competitions

The first competition among Scout Troops in Dunfermline was the Gibb Bugle competition introduced in 1916. This was won by the 1st Rosyth Scout Troop attached to Rosyth Navvy Mission (see page 15). The competition was not held again until 1923. Shortly afterwards other competitions were introduced – the Rotary Cup for first aid in 1925 and the Elder Cup for football. In 1935 the Millar Shield was donated for an annual sports meeting among Groups in the Rosyth area. Both Dunfermline and Rosyth Districts have trophies for sports, swimming, football, safety competitions and indoor inter-Troop meetings. A variety of other trophies have been competed for over the years including the Totem (the inter-Troop camping competition for Rosyth District) and the Mowgli Shield (an inter-Pack competition in Dunfermline District).

A County or Area Flag competition in Fife has been on the go for many years and West Fife Groups have had their share of success. Also at Area level the Cubs compete for the Darewski Cup (introduced in 1977) and the Venture Scouts have competed for the Benmore Challenge Shield. At national level there was a Scottish Challenge Hike (for Rovers/Venture Scouts) and in the late 1970s a Scottish inter-area competition was introduced in which Fife teams have excelled. Nowadays there are very few national competitions but when they did exist, West Fife Groups made their mark.

Winning competitions invites the taking of a commemorative photograph and there was plenty of choice in compiling this section. In making the selection, the aim has been to feature as many different competitions and Groups as possible.

Millar Shield 1935. A shield for a sports competition among Groups in Rosyth, Inverkeithing and North Queensferry was presented by Alex Millar of the 68th Fife (St Peter's Parish Church Inverkeithing) in 1935. The first winners were the 41st Fife (Rosyth) and here Mr Millar (left) is presenting the trophy to Group Scoutmaster Sam Clouston. The Millar Shield is still competed for today and is the oldest trophy in Rosyth District.

Cub Football League Shield 1936. The 52nd Fife (Red Triangle Rosyth) Pack won the league championship in 1936 and they are seen here outside their headquarters in Backmarch Road. The adult is probably Cubmaster Charles Dryden.

Foggo Memorial Trophy 1950. John Foggo, District Commissioner and Group Scout-master of the 2nd Fife (YMCA), died in 1949. He was a keen swimmer and the Foggo Memorial Trophy for life-saving was introduced the following year in his memory. Appropriately, the first winners were the 2nd Fife and their team is pictured here with the trophy. Seated (left) is R. Donn, standing J. Davidson and J. Robertson and seated right D. Halley. (Photo by Norval).

Rotary Cup c.1952. The Rotary Cup was used for different types of competition in its early days but soon became the trophy for an annual ambulance competition. This team from the 44th Fife (St Leonard's) won the Rotary Cup in 1952 or 1953 – left to right: John Livingstone; Bob Clough; George Tawse; Jack Anderson.

Totem Trophy 1953. When the Rosyth/Inverkeithing area formed its own Local Association in 1952, they introduced a number of new trophies for competition among Groups in the area. The Totem carved by James Graham of Inverkeithing High School was the trophy for the annual camping competition. The first winners were the 13th Fife (Rosyth Methodist) and Patrol Leader Terry Biles is seen here receiving the trophy from the leader of the examining team John Dewar, DC of Clackmannan District.

61st Fife with Trophies 1957. The 61st Fife (St John's RC Church Rosyth) with trophies won in 1957 – The Kennaway Cup (sports), Woolmer Trophy and Recorder Cup (ambulance). The leaders include Peter Jackson; Roy Ford; Rosalin Gaughan and Margaret Burke. Note the Pack Totem Pole at the back.

Inverkeithing District Sports 1957. Above – an action shot from the long jump competition at the Scout Sports held at Pitreavie in 1957. Cubs from the 13th Fife (Rosyth Methodist) are in the foreground and Dave Toshack, Ross Kerr and Willie Webster from the 41st Fife (Rosyth) are at the right hand edge. The Scouter wearing the raincoat is Kenny Moir of the 49th Fife (St Andrew and St George Church Rosyth). Below – Forbes Duncan, headmaster of Camdean School, Rosyth, presents the Patterson Trophy to the 41st Fife (Rosyth).

Gibb Bugle 1959. The team from the 44th Fife (St Leonard's) who won the Gibb Bugle competition in 1959. Left to right back row: John Ramsay; George Walker; Billy Hendry; George Walker; Stuart Mowbray. Front row: -?-; -?-; Alan Cameron. (Yes there were two Scouts called George Walker!)

Woolmer Trophy 1960. The team from the 13th Fife (Rosyth Methodist) in celebratory mood after winning the Woolmer Trophy competition (run on the basis of an indoor troop meeting). Left to right Malcolm Collens; David Black; Richard Bray; Tony Hollett; Sandy Collier and Hunter Logan.

68th Fife with Trophies 1962. The 68th Fife (St Peters Parish Church Inverkeithing Fife) won the Totem competition held at Broomhall in 1962. Above Patrol Leader Stuart Hay receives the Totem from Mr Graham of Kinross who led the examining team. To the left of Stuart is Mike Roberts of the 52nd. To the right of Mr Graham is Ted Hook, Scoutmaster of the 67th Fife. The team from the 68th Fife went on to win the County Flag competition. Below the team from the 68th Fife are pictured with their instructor and the Recorder Cup which they also won in 1962. Left to right back row: John Venters; Angus Whyte; Cameron Swailes. Front row: Tommy Wilson; Stuart Hay; Alex Thompson. The Group now wear the Erracht Cameron tartan but are seen here in their former Scout green neckerchiefs. The Recorder Cup came from the Cable Ship *Recorder* which was broken up at Charlestown. It was donated to Inverkeithing District and was used as a trophy for an annual ambulance competition.

Inverkeithing District's Cub Football Competition 1964. For many years Inverkeithing District ran an annual 11 a side knockout football competition for the Cub section. The winners in 1964 were the 13th Fife (Rosyth Methodist) and team captain Graham Jappy receives the trophy from Assistant District Commissioner John Prior. Looking on are Cub Instructor Malcolm Collens, Cubmaster Rev. Robert Collens and Assistant Cubmaster Mary Murray. Note another style of Pack Totem Pole on the right (compare with page 58).

Mowgli Shield 1966. The Mowgli Shield is an annual competition for Cub Packs in Dunfermline District. In 1966 the shield was won jointly by the 2nd Fife (YMCA) and 3rd Fife (British Legion) Packs. The members of the 2nd Fife team are pictured here with the shield – from left to right: Donald McKenzie; Keith Spowart; Colin Gordon; John Jackson; Malcolm Bruce and Stephen Japp. (Dunfermline Press).

Rotary Cup 1966. The team from the 39th Fife (St Margaret's) who won the Cup in 1966. A second team from the troop were runners up. Left to right back row: Ralph Cartwright; Russell Mann; James Simpson; Michael Romeling. Front row: Douglas Tulloch; Gordon McFarlane; Murray Laing; Eric Sneddon. (Dunfermline Press).

Inverkeithing District Sports 1966. This event was held at HMS Caledonia sports ground. District Chairman James Scott presents the Kennaway Cup to Douglas Swatton of the 13th Fife (Rosyth Methodist) with other members of the Group to the right of the flag pole – James Stevenson, James Hood and Michael Dally. To the left are Cubs, Scouts and supporters from the 61st Fife (St John's RC Church Rosyth). In the right foreground is District Commissioner John Prior.

Dunfermline District Football 1969. Three teams who took the honours in the Dunfermline District football competitions are pictured at Pitreavie Playing Fields in June 1969. At the back are the 13th Fife (Rosyth Methodist) who won the Scout league, in the middle are the 75th Fife (Carnock and Oakley) who won the Cub league and in the front the 2nd Fife (YMCA) Cubs who won the knock out competition.

Rosyth District five-a-side Football Competition 1973. As part of their 21st anniversary celebrations Rosyth District held a five-a-side football competition at Inverkeithing Youth and Community Wing. On the left are Scouts of the 49th Fife (Rosyth) who won the Scout competition and Scouts of the 41st Fife (Rosyth). On the right are Cubs of the 41st Fife and 61st Fife (St John's RC Church Rosyth) who were the finalists in the Cub competition. From the 41st Fife Venture Unit who organised the competition are Dave Webster, Mike Lambert, Gordon Stevenson, Jim Davidson and Brian Blanchflower. Kenny Thomson from Dunfermline Athletic FC presented the prizes. District Commissioner John Lyson is in the background.

Dunfermline District five-a-side Football 1982. The winning teams from the five-a-side football competitions in 1982. In the back row is the team from the 39th Fife who won the league – from left to right: Michael Stevens, Gordon Delaney, Michael Pugh, Alastair Wishart, Neil Stephen. In the middle row are the 26th Fife who won the knock out cup: Raymond Watson, Martin Overton, Martin Bell, Ian McConnell, Oswald Logan, Graham Corke. In the front the team from the 65th Fife who were the 2nd division league champions – Stewart Toshack, Colin Timms, Billy Teven, John Grieve, Ian Grieve. (Dunfermline Press)

Dunfermline Swimming Gala 1983. At the annual swimming gala the 39th Fife (St Margaret's) Troop won both the Hutton Challenge Trophy and the Foggo Memorial Trophy. With the trophies are left to right back row: Lindsay Short, Craig Scotland, Ian Gibb, Bryan Craig, Eric Connor. Front row David Hamilton, Grant Abbot, David Wilson. (Dunfermline Press).

Gibb Bugle Competition 1984. The competition was held at Fordell Firs and was run by Scouters from Rosyth District. Here Assistant District Commissioner Mike Lambert of 41st Fife (Rosyth) talks to the Scouts at the end of the competition. Behind him Jerry Pyke of 48th Fife (Dalgety Bay) is checking the points. Dunfermline's District Commissioner Rev Douglas Aitken stands by with the Gibb Bugle and Jim Tonner of the 75th Fife (Oakley) plays a supporting role with the District Flags. The team from the 44th Fife (St Leonard's) are at the right edge of the photograph.

Totem Competition 1984. Rosyth District's Totem competition took place on the same weekend at Fordell run by Scouters from Dunfermline District. District Commissioner John Lyson congratulates the winning team from the 41st Fife (Rosyth) with Mike Lambert and Scouts from the 48th Fife (Dalgety Bay) and 13th Fife (Rosyth Methodist) in the background.

114th Fife with Trophies 1985. The 114th Fife (Linburn) with the Rotary Cup and the five-a-side football knockout cup and league shield which they won in 1985. The team members are left to right back row: Andrew Aitken; Blair Higgins; David Hood. Front row: John Bruce; Andrew Paisley; William Perkins; Keith Chandler. (Dunfermline Press).

Rosyth District Sports 1985. Jimmy Spence of the 41st Fife (Rosyth) Scout Group presents the Andrew Wilson Memorial Trophy to Scouts of the 41st Fife – Scott Cameron and Derek Christie. Sports convener Jim Thompson looks on.

Rosyth District Sports 1989. Cubs and Scouts from the 13th Fife (Rosyth Methodist) with the Millar Shield and Clouston Cup won at the District Sports. Left to right back row: Martin Hall; David Payne; Peter MacGregor; Alan Connery; Nicky Mathieson; Paul Caudrey; Scott Pritchard; Ross Blyth; Jonathan Drever. Middle row: Lee Grindlay; Steven Caudrey; Fraser Craig; David Reid; Colin Johnstone; Stuart Wilson; Stuart Reid; Graeme Meiklejohn; Gary Connery. Front row: Douglas Grindlay; Niall Manson; Grant Ballantyne; Jamie Doctor; Gavin Byrne; Sean Reid; Scott Dow; Russell Craig; Stuart Meiklejohn; Ross Ballantyne.

Rosyth District Beaver Sports 1994. The Beavers gather at the end of their Sports Day. Assistant District Commissioner Elaine Pert of 48th Fife (Dalgety Bay) stands by the table as District Commissioner Bob Liddle at the right of the photograph announces the results.

Dunfermline District Sports 1997. Cubs of the 81st Fife (1st Broomhall) with the Cubs sports shield. Left to right: Adam Leszczuk; Elaine Renouf; Adam Hunter; Matthew Hutchings; Grant Corrie. The 81st Fife have regularly won this trophy in recent years.

13th Fife Scouts with Trophies 2000. A good year for the 13th Fife (Rosyth Methodist) Scouts with success in the Safety Totem and Woolmer Trophy competitions. Left to right back row: Mchael Collins; Michael Cunnae; Steven Hunter; James Garnett; Craig Hunter; Ross Leyman. Front row: Mark Penny; Euan Grindlay; Shannon McWilliam; Scott Brown; Chris Dewar.

Darnell Challenge Cup 1921. This was a Great Britain swimming competition with teams competing against the clock in their own areas and the results being sent to Headquarters for comparison. The 2nd Fife (YMCA) had a strong swimming tradition and won this trophy on four occasions – 1920, 1921, 1922 and 1925 and were runners up in 1923. Here we see the 1921 team with the Cup and wearing their individual medals. Left to right: Scout H. Moore; King's Scout Senior Patrol Leader J. Wright; Scout D. Morwood; Patrol Leader D. Ritchie (later to become District Commissioner). (Dunfermline Carnegie Library – Local History Collection).

County Flag 1949. It is unusual to see a photograph of a team in action during the competition but here we see the 13th Fife (Rosyth Methodist) team carrying a casualty on a stretcher during the 1949 competition held at Wemyss Firs. They went on to win the competition. Left to right Jimmy Hutchison (later of 81st Fife), John Brooks, Drummond Sharp, Donald Mackenzie with Pete Rutherford the unfortunate patient. The examining team were probably from the 87th Fife (HMS Caledonia) Rover Crew.

Duke of Connaught Shield 1951. Another national competition was the Duke of Connaught Shield for rifle shooting. The 2nd Fife (YMCA) entered teams for a number of years and were runners up in 1950, won the competition in 1951 and were placed third in 1953. This is the victorious 1951 team of R. Laing and A. Johnstone in the back row and D. Birrell and T. Grant in the front.

County Flag 1964. The winning team from the 44th Fife (St Leonard's) with the County Flag. Left to right back row: P. McKenna; Donald Dewar; John Ramsay; William Lang. Front row: Andrew Anderson; Ian Herd; C. McKenna. (Dunfermline Press).

Scottish Challenge Hike 1964. A team from the 2nd Fife (YMCA) won the Scottish Challenge Hike in 1964, completing a hat trick of successive wins for the Group. In recognition of their achievement they were allowed to retain the Challenge Hike Quaich. The winning team are seen with the Quaich at the Scottish Rover Moot at Borthwick Estate in June 1964 – left to right: Jock Baillie, Jimmy Cameron and Sandy Walker.

County Flag 1973. Another success for Dunfermline District with their representatives, 39th Fife (St Margaret's), winning the County Flag. Pictured here with the District Flags, the Gibb Bugle and the County Flag are left to right back row: John Lees; David Jolly; Craig Seath; Richard Gray. In front are Bryan Johnstone and Robert Bowie. (Dunfermline Press).

Scottish Orienteering Championship 1976. The 39th Fife (St Margaret's) won the Scout Junior Orienteering Competition held at Fordell Firs in May 1976. Back row left to right: Colin Jeffs; Craig Ebbage; Ewan Aitken; Scott McCallum. Front row: David Buchanan and Steven Jones. (Dunfermline Press).

Area Flag 1980. The 41st Fife (Rosyth) won the Area Flag in 1980 and went on to win the Inter – Area Camping competition, the first time the competition had been won by a Fife team. The team are, left to right: James Bayne; Martin Campbell; John Smith; Peter Scrimegeour; Gordon Macari; Campbell McDermid.

Clean Up Champions 1981. As part of Scout Job Week a national clean up competition was run sponsored by Kentucky Fried Chicken. The Scottish Champions in 1981 (and in later years) were the 39th Fife (St Margaret's). Representatives of the Group (and Area) are pictured here at Scottish Headquarters receiving their prize. Left to right, back row: Ross McArthur; Alan Short; Deputy Area Commissioner, Jack Cowieson; Bert Hayhoe; Neil Stephen; Lindsay Short; Tom Salmon; Ken Marshall; Andy Hamilton. Front row: Graeme McIntyre; Stuart Christie; Barry Hailstones; Richard Cunningham; Ewan Venters; Ian Sneddon; Alastair Pryde.

Inter-Area Camping Competition 1982. It was Dunfermline District's turn to represent Fife in the Inter-Area competition in 1982 as their representatives, 114th Fife (Linburn), had won the Area Flag. The team were placed second in the overall competition but won the Coca-Cola Cup awarded for certain parts of the competition. Left to right: Gordon Chamberlain; Alistair Matson; Paul Stephen; Blair Higgins; Duncan Kerr with Derek Bell holding the trophy. (Dunfermline Press)

Darewski Cup 1982. The competition was run in conjunction with the activities organised for the visit of Chief Scout Michael Walsh to Lochore Meadows. For the first (and only time) Rosyth District won the cup and Assistant District Commissioner Sarah Giles is pictured above holding the cup. Behind her are leaders from the 49th Fife (Rosyth) including Bill Green and Linda Sherwood. Below, Sarah is pictured with Captain David Fairlie, Area Commissioner; Dorothy Kinloch, Chief Commissioner for Scotland; John Lyson, District Commissioner for Rosyth District, and Jean Jeffries, Assistant Area Commissioner (Cubs).

Inter-Area Camping Competition 1983. Having again won the Area Flag competition in 1983, a team from the 114th Fife (Linburn) went one better (see page 74) by winning the Inter-Area competition. Their prize was a patrol tent donated by Vango. Left to right Derek Bell; Mark Hood; Blair Higgins; John Bruce; Paul Stephen; Duncan Kerr. (Dunfermline Press).

Area Flag 1984. Completing a hat trick of wins for Dunfermline District in the Area Flag competition of 1984 was the team from the 39th Fife (St Margaret's). Left to right: Graeme McIntyre; Craig Scotland; Bryan Craig; Ian Gibb; David Hamilton; David Wilson. (Dunfermline Press).

Six

Chief Scouts' Visits/ International Scouting

The founder of the Scout Movement, Sir Baden-Powell (as he was then), and his wife visited Dunfermline on 3 September 1917 and addressed a Rally of Scouts and Guides in Pittencrieff Park. Sadly there is no known photograph of that occasion. A Scottish Rally was held on 24 June 1933 at South Inch Perth to meet Lord Baden-Powell. It was to be twenty-one years before a Chief Scout (Lord Rowallan) met Fife Scouts at a rally at Raith Estate, Kirkcaldy and a further twelve years before his successor, Sir Charles Maclean, attended a rally of Fife Scouts at Glenrothes Airfield. Visits from Chief Scouts became more frequent after that at intervals of between five and eight years. The first part of this section captures some moments from these visits.

In the early days of Scouting, the opportunity to meet Scouts from other countries was limited. The World Jamborees held every four years gave this opportunity to a small number of Scouts and the presence in Dunfermline of the College of Physical Education brought some foreign Scouters to Dunfermline. However, it is only in the last forty years or so that wider opportunities have existed for Scouts in West Fife to go abroad or attend international events. At home the biennial Blair Atholl Jamborettes (which began in 1946) are one such opportunity and a number of Scout Groups have used the International Scout Centres at Kandersteg and Wiltz. Some Groups have entered teams in the Explorer Belt expeditions. The second part of this section has a small selection of the many international camps and events in which West Fife Scouts have taken part.

Lord Baden-Powell of Gilwell OM, GCMG
1908-1941

Lord Somers KCMG, DSO, MC
1941-1944

Lord Rowallan KT, KBE, MC, TD, LLD, DL
1945-1959

Lord Maclean KT, GCVO, KBE
1959-1971

Sir William Gladstone Bt, DL, MA
1972-1982

Major-General Michael J.H. Walsh CB, DSO
1982-

Chief Scouts 1908-1988. This composite postcard produced in the early 1980s shows the first six Chief Scouts. There is no record of Lord Somers visiting Dunfermline or Fife but all of the others have done so on one or more occasions. (courtesy of The Scout Association & Scout Shops Ltd).

Lord Baden-Powell in Perth, 1933. This photograph of Lord Baden-Powell is thought to have been taken at the Scottish Rally in Perth in June 1933.

Lady Baden-Powell in Dunfermline 1948. This was a Girl Guide and not a Scouting occasion and strictly does not belong in this book. However, I could not resist the temptation of including this photograph of Lady Baden-Powell on a visit to the Youth Centre in Dunfermline on 27 October 1948. Seated (left) is Miss J.B. Buchanan (Divisional Commissioner for Central Fife). Standing left to right: Miss E.M. Beveridge (County Camp Adviser); Netta Dick (Youth Leader); Miss M.M. Cowan (Divisional Secretary for West Fife) and Miss E.O. Black (County Ranger Adviser).

Lord Rowallan is pictured here at the rally at Raith Estate, Kirkcaldy on 13 June 1964. On the left is Assistant District Commissioner Abe Johnston and on the right District Commissioner Duncan Ritchie.

Sir Charles Maclean at Glenrothes 1966. A Rally was held at Glenrothes Airfield on 28 May. Sir Charles made his way round the large circle of Cubs and (above) he is seen talking to Brian Henderson of the 2nd Fife (YMCA). During the rally he presented the Silver Acorn to County Commissioner Abe Johnston (below) who was retiring from the post. (Dunfermline Press).

Commemorative Badges. For Sir Charles Maclean's visit in 1966, a souvenir pennant was produced as pennants rather than badges were the norm in those days. For subsequent Chief Scouts' visits, commemorative badges were produced although only in more recent times could these be worn on uniform. The range of badges from 1974 to date are shown here.

Sir William Gladstone at Fordell 1974. Sir William's visit to Fife Scouts was coupled with a visit to the National Cub Day at Fordell Firs on 8 June. The Fife Cubs and Scouts assembled in a field near Fordell and above we see a welcome to the Chief from the Cubs with Assistant County Commissioner Jean Jeffries and County Commissioner Captain David Fairlie directing proceedings. Below Sir William chats to David Fairlie. (Dunfermline Press).

The Rally to greet Major.-General Michael Walsh was held at Lochore Meadows on 12 June 1982. Above he is seen with Area Commissioner Captain David Fairlie and Scouts and Venture Scouts from Fife who had gained awards including Robert Bowie, 39th Fife (St Margaret's), on the left. He was asked to put his foot in a tray of earth so that a plaster cast could be made, as shown below. Joe Rosiejak, Stuart Gibb and Scouts of the 39th Fife look on. (Dunfermline Press).

A site at Balcormo near Leven was the setting for the first visit of Garth Morrison as Chief Scout on 4 June 1989. Above he is visiting the Rosyth District site and talking to District Commissioner Bob Liddle with Area Commissioner Frank Hood looking on. In the foreground are the District Beavers with Beaver Leader Jean Shaw of the 13th Fife (Rosyth Methodist). In the background organising activities are Cub Leaders Bill King, Walter Punton and David Boath from the 41st Fife (Rosyth); David Dykes, 61st Fife (St John's RC Rosyth); and Martin Stephen, 68th Fife (St Peter's Parish Church Inverkeithing). Below he is visiting the Dunfermline District site with Area Commissioner Frank Hood, District Commissioner Ken Marshall and Bob Craig, 39th Fife (St Margaret's). The Scouts are from the 44th Fife (St Leonard's) and include Douglas Anderson, Raymond Fagan and David Baxter.

Garth Morrison at Dalgety Bay 1994. Garth Morrison is the only Chief Scout to have made two official visits to Fife Scouts. His second visit was to a site near Dalgety Bay on 5 June. Above – accompanied by Peter Merckel 48th Fife (Dalgety Bay), he is chatting to members of the 13th Fife (Rosyth Methodist) – Cub Scout Leader Martin Rogers; Beaver Leader Jean Shaw; Cubs Alan Stewart and Dugald West and Venture Scout Paul Ward. With his back to the camera is District Chairman David Hill and in the background is Dot Wright of the 41st Fife (Rosyth). Below he is presenting awards to Scouts and Venture Scouts from the 62nd Fife (Crossford) and 114th Fife (Linburn) Groups.

The Rally to meet George Purdie was held at Fordell Firs on 20 June 1999. Above he is entering the Rosyth District campsite accompanied by District Commissioner Alan Bull. Below he is at one of the activities in the Dunfermline District site. Area Commissioner Danny Barr is in the background.

Links with Trondheim, Norway 1946. At the end of the war the youth of Dunfermline 'adopted' the town of Trondheim in Norway. In 1945, the Scouts of Dunfermline sent the Scouts of Trondheim a St Andrew's Flag and a football. In August 1946 a party of young people from Trondheim had a short holiday in Dunfermline and during this visit Rover Scout Roar Wist presented District Commissioner Major R.P. Easton with a leather bound album containing a description and photographs of the handing over of the flag. The presentation was made during a visit to the 2nd Fife (YMCA) hut on Cults Hill.

Fife Contingent for Jamboree in France 1947. This is thought to be the Fife contingent of Scouts attending the Jamboree in France who are waiting to board a train at Dunfermline Lower Station. At the back under the signal is Marcus Johnston of the 2nd Fife (YMCA) and second from the right is another Scout from the 2nd Fife – John Gardener. The Scout third from the right is Frankie Miller from the 41st Fife (Rosyth).

Visit to Bavaria 1958. District Commissioner Abe Johnston took a party of ten Scouts from Dunfermline District to be the guests of a Scout Troop in Bavaria in 1958. After being given a civic reception in the town of Wurzburg the Scouts gave this demonstration of Scottish country dancing in the street outside.

Explorer Belt 1964. From 1960, the 2nd Fife (YMCA) regularly entered teams (of two) in the annual Explorer Belt expeditions which involved an extended hike of about ten days in a foreign country carrying out assignments en route. Only a small number of those taking part were awarded Explorer Belts. The 2nd Fife's first success was in 1964 when four of their Rovers (Gordon Brown, Douglas Anderson, John Robertson and David Strachan) were awarded belts. Here David and John show off their belts.

Danish Scouts in Dunfermline 1973. A party of Danish Scouts visited Dunfermline in 1973 as guests of the 44th Fife (St Leonard's) and 40th Fife (Touch) Scout groups. After a wet week at Auchengillan they enjoyed home hospitality in Dunfermline which included a Civic Reception from Dunfermline Town Council. They are pictured in the City Chambers with local Scouts and Provost Les Wood. At the top of the picture are District Commissioners Syd King and John Lyson, at the bottom left is Roddy Adamson of the 40th Fife and on the right are Ian Quinn, Andy Hamilton (44th), Charlie Steedman (40th) and Bill Cook (44th).

44th Fife in Luxembourg 1979. A party of Scouts from the 44th Fife (St Leonard's) travelled to Wiltz in Luxembourg. Among those identified in this photograph are left to right back row: Alan Thomson; Bill Cook and Danny Barr; on the left of the second back row are Stuart Middleton and Ian Derrick, both from 114th Fife (Linburn) and Jack Knapman; at the right end of the second front row is Ian Ireland; in the front row are Fiona Ireland, on the left; John Robertson, fourth from left; Malcolm Cook, third from right; Derek Devlin, second from right.

2nd Fife in Luxembourg 1982. In 1982, the 2nd Fife (YMCA) also visited Wiltz. Left to right back row: -?-; David Ford; -?-; -?-. Second back row: Graham Scoon; Graham Ford; David Hutton; David Harris; Douglas Hutton; -?-; -?-; Gary Walker; -?-. Second front row: Ron Ford; -?-; -?-; -?-; Graham McCallum; -?-; -?-; ? Fraser; -?-. Front row: Tom Simpson; -?-; -?-; -?-; -?-; Euan Hutton; Ewan Aird; -?-.

Explorer Belt 1987. Five Venture Scouts from 39th Fife (St Margaret's) took part in the Scottish Explorer Belt expedition to Iceland. They are seen here with their Belts. Left to right back row: Iain Gibb, Lesley Craig and Lindsay Short. Front row: Donald Smith and Bryan Craig.

40th Fife in Austria c.1989. Members of the 40th Fife (Touch) are pictured outside their accommodation in Stanzach, Austria. Left to right back row: Roddy Adamson; Betty Barton; Jonathan Burns; Lee Byrnes; James Brown; Harry Campbell; Paul Grant; Alistair McGregor, 41st Fife; ? Blakey; ? Bradley; Barry Parnell; Keith Nisbet; Trish Heywood. Middle row: John Wilson; Gordon Mayze; Scott Brown; Barry McEwan; Graeme Inglis; Steven Duncan; Scott Hunter; Ian Barton; Allan Mellon. Front row: Gary Hunter; Neil Anderson; Barry McHale; -?-.

In 1994, the 44th Fife (St Leonard's) organised a trip to Luxembourg and other Groups were invited to take part. Here they are setting off on their journey. On the left are Danny Barr, Bill Cook and John Robertson.

68th Fife Trip to Finland/Sweden 1998. A group of Scouts from the 68th Fife (St Peter's Parish Church Inverkeithing) outside their Group headquarters. They are about to set off on a trip to Finland via Sweden. Left to right back row: Kevin Lloyd; Stuart Moy; Michael Macdonald; Alison Lloyd; Gary Dignam; Ian Reid. Middle row: Ben Morris; Ishbel Moy; Lynsey Moodie; Danielle Dingwall; David Dingwall. Front row: Chris ?; Sharron Woodward; Lee?

81st Fife and 3rd Fife in Holland 2000. A party of Scouts from the 81st Fife (1st Broomhall) and 3rd Fife (Royal British Legion) en route to an international gathering in Dronten, Holland.

Seven

Camping & Out of Doors

A main attraction of Scouting has always been the camping and outdoor activities and leaders are encouraged not to forget the 'OUT' in ScOUTing. This section features a number of different Colonies, Pack and Troops in camp or enjoying outdoor activities. It is interesting to note the changes in camp wear and equipment over the years. See also the earlier camp photographs included at pages 11-20.

41st Fife (Rosyth) in Camp in the late 1930s. Left to right standing:- Norrie Douglas; Willie McRearie; -?-; Tommy Ogg; -?-; -?-; -?-; -?-; David Hill (later District Chairman); -?-. Front row: -?-; Jack Hill; Jackie Spears; -?-; -?-.

13th Fife in Camp 1944. In 1940, Dunfermline District bought the former Miners' Welfare Institute in Lassodie for use as a District campsite. This is the only photograph I have found of the centre taken when the 13th Fife (Rosyth Methodist) were in residence in 1944. Only some of the names of those in the photograph are recorded and these are left to right standing: Ralph Collier; Dave Collier; John Brown; David Baker; Charles Billinness; Roy Whiting; William Sharp;-?-; -?-; ? Schoenenberger; -?-; -?-; -?-; -?-.

41st Fife Camp 1948. Parents Days were a feature of summer camps of the past and these are visitors to the camp of the Ogg Troop of the 41st Fife (Rosyth) held at Lockerbie in 1948 with Felix Hudson(?) second from the left. A bus was hired and relatives and friends would have a day's outing visiting the camp. The Scouts always looked forward to the 'goodies' brought by their parents to supplement (or perhaps replace) the camp cooking. It was also a time when homesickness came to a head and the bus sometimes had extra passengers going home!

75th Fife (Oakley) in Camp at Callander in 1949. Left to right back row: Jim Tonner; Jim Matson; Alex ?; Neil Young; Campbell Hamilton; Tom Lark; -?-; David Allan; Ronnie Brown; Willie Hepburn. Second row: Jim Buchanan; -?-; George Cowan; -?-; -?-. Front row: -?-; ? Clark; Billy ? Briggs; -?-; -?-. Lying down -?-; -?-.

26th Fife (Viewfield Baptist) Troop in camp at Almondbank in 1950. Left to right back row: Jimmy Jamieson; Bob Irvine; -?-; Ken Kyle; Abel Rees; Rev T. Gardner; Peter Robertson. Second back row: Derek Butchart; ? Black; John Paterson; Norman Burns; -?-; -?-; Andy Wilson. Second front row: Pete Atherton; Bobby Ferguson; George Primrose; James Hain; -?-; ? Barbour. Front row Andrew Jamieson; -?-; ? Peacock; -?-; -?-; -?-.

3rd Fife (British Legion) in Camp at Kilconquhar in 1951 with some members of the 77th Fife (Kelty). Left to right back row -?-; -?-; Eddie Mapstone; ? Lingwood; Tom Nairn; Tom Franklin; George Munro (77th); Fred Lingwood; Ian Reddie; Bob Mapstone; Willie Patterson (in white shirt); Peter Franklin; -?-; Tom Smart. Others identified – Alex Hunter (second from left in second back row); Bob Smart (in front of Ian Reddie); Willie Hynd? (in front of George Munro); Harvey Lingwood (the Cub sitting on the grass on the right); Jim? McGowan (behind Harvey); Willie Robertson (kneeling on grass in front of Peter Franklin).

41st Fife with Trek Cart *c.*1952. A patrol of Scouts from the 41st Fife (Rosyth) en route to the Gibb Bugle competition. Left to right: Jimmy Rennie; Tony Knight (?); Ian Patterson; Mike Hudson (?); -?-; -?-. The photograph was taken at the beginning of the dual carriageway to Dunfermline near the Pitreavie Cottages. This section of road has since disappeared under the Pitreavie roundabout.

The 13th Fife (Rosyth Methodist) Troop had a favourite camp site at the old quarry near Cleish and they are pictured there at their annual camp in 1953. Left to right, back row Alan Lucas; Cyril Blackburn; Terry Biles; Steven Foster; Brian Hollett; John Roxburgh; Jimmy Hutchison; Donald Mackenzie. Middle row: Pete Roxburgh; Terry Hyde, John Brown; Ron Woolmer; -?-; -?- . Front row: Dave Patterson; Bill Shore, Ray Lawrence; Alf Barns; John Braybrooke; Alun John; Dougie Young.

3rd Fife in Camp 1954. The 3rd Fife (British Legion) in camp at Lochearnhead in 1954. Left to right, back row: Davie (?) Peattie; Tom Smart; Abe Johnston; Bob Haxton; Willie Robertson. Second back row: (on left) Jim Ditchburn; Harvey Lingwood; Rob Smart – (on right) Bob Stenhouse (former Scoutmaster); Syd King; -?-; Ed Mapstone. At the right front is Fred Lingwood with Peter Franklin behind him. A number of the unidentified boys are French Scouts.

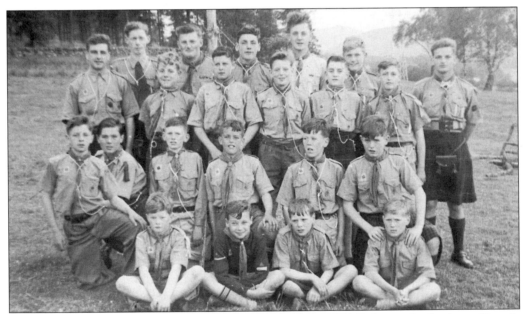

44th Fife (St Leonard's) in Camp at Pitlochry, probably in 1956. Left to right, back row Dougie Ireland; Bob Clough; Harry Hamilton; Bruce Thompson; Billy Hendry; Roy Hunter (in kilt). Second back row: Andy Hamilton; Dave Cuthbertson; Jimmy Scott; -?-; Raymond Bramber; Sandy Morris. Second front row: Billy Hynd; -?-; Gordon Currie; George Walker; Ian Adamson; Alex Ramsay. Front row: ? McArthur; Colin McKenzie; Bill Cook;-?-.

65th Fife in Camp *c.*1960. Scouts from the 65th Fife (Brucefield) in camp probably about 1960. Jimmy Scotland is third from the left in the back row and Alex Petrie is fourth from the left.

75th Fife (Oakley) on a hike in the early 1960s. Some scouts from the 75th Fife (Oakley) Troop on a hike whilst camping in the Loch Lomond area. At the back of the group is George Tonner and on the right John Young.

Strathkinness Youth House. Fife County Council ran a Youth House in Strathkinness which was available to youth groups for camps etc. It was a popular venue for Cub pack holidays and was also used for training courses. A fire put an end to its use for this purpose. This photograph was taken in 1975.

A group of Cubs from various Packs in Inverkeithing District during a pack holiday at Strathkinness Youth House in 1965. The leaders in the back row include Billy Gresty 13th Fife (Rosyth Methodist); Bill Giles 67th Fife (North Queensferry); Tom Pearson 13th Fife; John Lyson 41st Fife (Rosyth) and Sarah Giles 67th Fife.

61st Fife (St John's RC Rosyth) in Camp at Menstrie near Alva, in the late 1960s. Third from the right in the back row is Roy Ford and the casualty in the front row (with a broken arm) is John Glackin.

104th Fife (Holy Trinity) in Camp at Milton by Saline in 1968. Left to right back row: Graeme Kay; Reggie Vaughan; Bob Sinclair; Stephen Owen; Robin Ozog; Phil Smithard. Middle row: Brian Heggie; Gordon Munroe; Michael Stark; David Brown. Front row: -?-; Paul Boarer; -?-; Timmy Owen; ? Burke; Martin Burke.

68th Fife (St Peter's Parish Church, Inverkeithing) in Camp at Gosforth Park 1977. Left to right: Iain McCormick; Duncan McCormick; Raymond Scott; Timothy Carpenter; Thomas Scott; Kevin Gray; Brian Harrower; Andrew Geddes.

68th Fife Scouts Hillwalking c.1979. A group of Scouts from 68th Fife (St Peter's Parish Church Inverkeithing) have a break while on a hill walking expedition in Scotland. Left to right: Kevin Lloyd; -?-; Iain McCormick (?); Peter Bastianelli; Andrew Geddes; Kevin Gray; -?-.

48th Fife Scouters 1981. A relaxed (but synchronised) group of Scouters from the 48th Fife (Dalgety Bay) at the Troop's camp at Bridge of Allan in 1981. Left to right: Jerry Pyke; Gordon Pert; John Houston and Tom Mitchell.

39th Fife Beavers Sausage Sizzle 1982. The newly formed Beaver Colony attached to the 39th Fife (St Margaret's) enjoy a sausage sizzle in the grounds of their headquarters. The leaders are Lesley Craig (on left) and Linda Langskaill.

13th Fife Beavers at Dollar 1984. Some of the 13th Fife (Rosyth Methodist) Beavers visiting the Cubs, who were on a pack holiday at Brewlands Outdoor Centre, Dollar. Left to right: Martin Hall; Scott Pritchard; -?-; Stephen Kirk; -?-; -?-; Andrew Patrick (?); -?-; Paul Ward; -?-; -?-; -?-; Terry O'Neill; -?-; Tony Bilton; Robert McCluskey; -?-; Martin King; Gary Connery. (Photo by John Shaw)

39th Fife Visit HMS Beaver 1985. The visit of HMS Beaver to Rosyth Dockyard in November 1985 gave local Beaver Colonies the chance to visit the ship. Beavers (and Cubs) from the 39th Fife (St Margaret's) are pictured here beside the ship with leaders Alex Smith and Linda Langskaill.

Inch Scout Fellowship in Raft Race 1987. A team from the Inch Scout Fellowship in Rosyth District in the Kenmore-Aberfeldy raft race in June 1987. Front to back, starboard side: -?-; Kenny Moyes; -?-; Kevin Lloyd. Port side: Colin Gardener; Gary Dignam; Kevin Hughes; Steven Don.

49th Fife Cubs in Camp 1988. Cubs from the 49th Fife (Rosyth) on an outing to Pitlochry in 1988 while camping in the area. The leaders are Lee Symms and Wally Walton.

61st Fife Cubs Visit Coronation Street 1997. While on a Pack Holiday in North Yorkshire, these Cubs from the 61st Fife (St John's RC Church Rosyth) visited Coronation Street. Left to right, back row: Helen McMahon, David Dykes; Catherine Walker; Julie Dykes. Front row: Christopher Plascott; Iain Dykes; Rikky Salmond; Scott Walker; Lee Chapman; Gary Stevenson; Mary McMahon. (Photo by Granada Studios).

81st Fife at Lochgoilhead 1998. Cubs and Scouts from the 81st Fife (1st Broomhall) at the National Scout Boating Centre at Lochgoilhead. The four nearest the camera left to right are Grant Corrie; John McMorran; Abby McMurtrie and Jordan Crawford.

Eight
Special Occasions etc.

Most of the photographs in this Section are of presentations of one kind or another – awards, farewell gifts, new colours (flags). A number of other photographs were taken at Scout Group reunions. The remainder are of groups or individuals which did not fit into any of the other Sections of the book but which were worthy of inclusion.

61st Fife *c.*1930. An early photograph of the 61st Fife (St John's RC Rosyth). Left to right back row: R. McNeil; M. Burns; J. Bryce; E. Callaghan; P. Northcote; ? Robjohns; J. McDonald. Second back row: ? Kelly; V. Garland; ? Baker; ? O'Connor; Bruce McColville; ? O' Hanlon. Second front row: ? Ward; John Horne; Ned Burke; Harold Jackson; Father Hart; William Collins; Mr McGonigle; Mr Robjohns and J. McDonald. Front row: ? Power; J Brady; Robert Duffy; Donald Tazioli; Peter Jackson; ? O'Connor; Angus Duffy; ? Northcote; L. Garland; B. Watters; P. Lynch; J. Baker.

John Leask Aberdour *c.*early 1930s. John Leask was the first Group Scoutmaster of the 66th Fife (St Fillan's Aberdour) which was founded in 1933. He had had a long involvement with the Scout Movement having been Scoutmaster of the 4th Leith from at least 1913 and also District Commissioner of Leith District for a time. It is not known when this photograph was taken but it may well have been in his early days with the Aberdour Group.

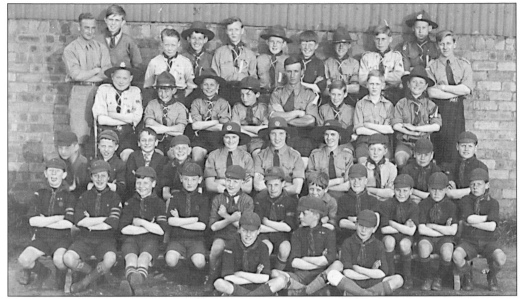

52nd Fife *c*.1935. A Group photograph of the 52nd Fife (Red Triangle Club) taken around 1935. Left to right, back row: Ian Shaw; Bert Dally; Douglas Sandison; John Carlton; Ian Wilson; Andrew Jubb (?); -?-; Gordon Smith; -?-; Gilbert Sandison; John Wallace. Second back row: Tom Sandison; Gordon Wilson; -?-; -?-; Andy Wilson; -?-; -?-; Frank Banner. Middle Row: Margaret Simmons (?), 6th from left, and Freddy Buchanan (?), on the right. Second front row: Jackie Stonnar; Duncan Stewart; Malcolm Cameron (?); -?-; Benny Richards; Johnny Burney; -?-; Isaac Richards (?); Norman Nekrews; -?-; Harry Buchanan. Front row: Bobby Mann; Harry McIvor; Hugh Taylor.

39th Fife *c*.1942. An early photograph of the 39th Fife (St Margaret's) Troop. In the second back row are John Graham on the left; Rev. William Steven; David Rowe, on the right.

81st Fife c.1946. Members of the 81st Fife (1st Broomhall) at their Christmas party in either 1946 or 1947. Left to right in the back row are: Jim Brown; Tom Brown; Bill Carty; -?-; -?-; -?-; -?-; -?-; Hamish Kerr.

2nd Fife Reunion 1948. For many years the 2nd Fife (YMCA) held a reunion dinner at the beginning of the year. This is the reunion of 1948 held in the Bruce Street hall. (Photo by Peter Leslie).

41st Fife 1949. The members of the 41st Fife (Rosyth) Ogg Troop in January 1949. Left to right back row: Willie Webster; Dave Smith; George McFarlane; B. Roberts (?); Alex McGowan; Alan Lightly; Dave Tannock. Middle row: Albert Barrow; Ian Allardyce; Trevor Fairlamb; Billy Gow; Dave Webster; Leslie Shears. Front row: Ben Kent (kneeling); Norrie Douglas; Felix Hudson; Frank Pope; Roy Benzie (kneeling).

3rd Fife Anniversary Reunion 1950. This reunion was held by the 3rd Fife (British Legion) to mark their 25th anniversary. Among those standing are Fred Lingwood; Willie Robertson; Bob Mapstone; Ronan Scott and Peter Franklin. The Scouters etc seated are left to right: Ed Mapstone; Frank Mathieson; George Moyes; Willie Alexander; Eddie Thomson; Syd King; George Munro 77th; -?-; Willie Patterson; Ian Reddie. (Photo by Peter Leslie).

Inverkeithing & District Flag 1953. In 1952, a separate Inverkeithing Local Association was formed for Scout Groups in Rosyth, Inverkeithing and North Queensferry. A district flag was designed and painted by Derek Seymour based on the coat of arms of the Burgh of Inverkeithing. Although it bears the date 1953 it was dedicated at the annual St George's Day Parade in 1955. The flag is now laid up in St Peter's Parish Church in Inverkeithing.

41st Fife Queen's Scout 1955. Troop Leader Iain Craig of the 41st Fife (Rosyth) receives his Queen's Scout certificate from County Commissioner Maj. Crichton-Stuart in November 1955.

41st Fife Group Committee 1957. In the 1950s, many Scout Groups formed Group Committees to help with the fundraising etc required to support Scouting. These are some of the ladies of the 41st Fife (Rosyth) Group Committee at some function in February 1957. Left to right: Nancy Black, Bess Kidd, Mrs L Smith, Edie French and Ann McIntosh.

Presentation of Colours to 96th Fife 1957. The colours of the 96th Fife (Canmore Congregational Church) were dedicated in March 1957. Left to right Douglas Watt; Kemp Blyth; Doug Watson; Rev. A. McDougall; Robert Hall; Martin Lowe; Stewart Drummond.

Dunfermline District Executive Committee 1957. This photograph was taken for a Dunfermline Press article on the Scout Association's Golden Jubilee. In those days Groups were represented on the Executive Committee by a Scouter and a lay person. Left to right standing: Bert Elliot, 75th Fife (Oakley); Joe Kirkhouse, 26th Fife (Viewfield Baptist); John Young (?), 75th Fife; Donald (?) Mackenzie, 97th Fife (St Margaret's RC); George Munro, 77th Fife (Kelty Oakfield); -?-; Donald Cameron; Duncan ?, 77th Fife; Peter Richardson, 2nd Fife (YMCA); ? Smart; Willie Robertson, 3rd Fife (British Legion); Willie Scott, 44th Fife (St

Leonard's); James Wilson, 2nd Fife; ? Macpherson (?); Simon Hunter, 2nd Fife; -?-; -?-; Duncan Ritchie, Honorary District Commissioner. Front row: William Collins, 97th Fife; Willie Alexander, Warrants Secretary; Davie Rodger, 46th Fife (Cowdenbeath YMCA); Eddie Thomson, Assistant District Commissioner; Abe Johnston, District Commissioner; Ronald Stevenson, Chairman; John Thomson, Secretary; Janet Strang, 39th Fife (St Margaret's Parish); R. Page Young, Treasurer.

13th Fife Tree Planting 1957. A number of Groups in Inverkeithing District planted trees to mark the Scout Movement's 50th anniversary in 1957. The 13th Fife (Rosyth Methodist) planted two trees in the front of their Church in Parkgate. Left to right back row: John Roxburgh, Bill Shore, Tony Hollett, Alun John, Cyril Blackburn, Keith Butler and Jane Roxburgh. Front row: Brian Heritage, Sandy Collier, Hunter Logan, -?-, Sandy Collier, Gordon Ferguson, Billy Gresty, Chris Colmer, Donald Hunter, Maldwyn Stride and Martin Rogers.

Presentation late 1950s. Little is known about this photograph. It appears to have been taken to mark the presentation of an award, probably a Queen's Scout Badge, and the Troop seems to have been either the 77th Fife (Kelty Oakfield) or the 46th Fife (Cowdenbeath YMCA). Fourth from the left in the middle row is George Munro of the 77th Fife and the three men in kilts are Abe Johnston, acting County Commissioner; Carl(ton) Tinn and Davie Rodger of the 46th Fife.

2nd Fife Wood Badge c.late 1950s. James Archibald of the 2nd Fife (YMCA), later District Commissioner, is presented with the Wood Badge by District Commissioner Abe Johnston. In the background is the bronze plaque in memory of David Allan, the founder of the 2nd Fife Scout Troop.

Presentation of Queen's Scout Badges 1960. Until 1968, the highest award a Scout could gain was the Queen's Scout. No fewer than three members of the 41st Fife (Rosyth) are receiving their badges from District Commissioner Andy Wilson. Left to right they are Victor Letters, Ross Kerr (later of 114th Fife) and Neil Murray. (Photo by Peter Leslie).

Founder members of 114th Fife 1965. Recruits for the newly formed 114th Fife (Linburn) Scout Group in the Miners' Welfare Institute, Woodmill Road in May or June 1965. In the middle row is Douglas (?) Grindlay, second from left, and Archie Aitken, second from right. In the front row is Charles (?) Grindlay, left, and Derek Dowds, right.

3rd Fife Group 1965. This photograph of the 3rd Fife (British Legion) was taken at the time of the opening of their new headquarters in May 1965. Left to right back row: -?-; Jim Crosbie; ? Johnstone; -?-; -?-; -?-; ? McGowan; ? McCord; ? Cook; Brian Neaves. Second back row: John Turner; -?-; -?-; -?-; David King; -?-; -?-; John Anderson. Scouters seated: R. Cummings; W. McIntosh; Janette Lewis; Willie Robertson; Syd King; Margaret King; Alan Webb; Jimmy Bishop; G. Spence.

Presentation at 3rd Fife 1971. Anthony Mockett of the 3rd Fife (British Legion) receives the Chief Scout's Award certificate from Honorary County Commissioner Abe Johnston. Looking on are members of the team who won the Foggo Memorial Trophy at Dunfermline District's swimming gala along with leaders Dave King and Ian Mason. (Dunfermline Press).

Presentation to Rear Admiral Ridley 1972. For many years the Admiral Superintendent of the Dockyard was the Honorary President of Rosyth District. Rear Admiral Ridley was one of the longest serving Admirals Superintendent and was presented with a shield in appreciation of his services to the District. Making the presentation is District Chairman Dennis Crabbe. On the left of the back row is former District Commissioner John Prior and on the right District Commissioner John Lyson. Left to right in the front row are Mike Lafferty, then 49th Fife (St Andrew and St George Rosyth); Wilma Shanks and Willie Schopps, both of 48th Fife (Dalgety Bay) and Keith Butler, 13th Fife (Rosyth Methodist). (Dunfermline Press).

Presentation to Kenneth Turnbull 1975. Capt. David Fairlie presents the Queen's Scout certificate to Kenneth Turnbull of the 41st Fife (Rosyth). Left to right back row: Dave Webster; Alistair McGregor; Brian Blanchflower; -?-; Ross Kerr; Jim Davidson; Lewis Hudson; Ernie Blair; Ian Blair; Brian Davidson and John Linsell. Middle row: Isabel Ross; Sandy Campbell; Mike Lambert; Gordon Stevenson; John Lyson and Jimmy Spence. The Scout in the front is Iain Webster.

Chief Scout's Award Presentations 40th Fife 1978. Scouts of the 40th Fife (Touch) with their Chief Scout's Award certificates. Left to right Kenneth Horn; John McCord; David Moffat; David Birrell; Colin Watson; James Turner. In the back row is Group Scout Leader Rod Adamson with the first female recruits to the Group's Venture Unit – Heather ?; -?-. Lyn Pratt; Shona Campbell; Dawn Gibb; Sylvia Whitehill; Arlene Nellis; ? Sharp; -?-; Catrina Whitelaw.

District Badges 1978. In 1978 Dunfermline and Rosyth Districts introduced District Badges – the first in Fife, if not Scotland. The Dunfermline badge features the east elevation of Dunfermline Abbey. The Rosyth badge is loosely based on the Inverkeithing coat of arms with the ship symbolising the links which the communities in the District have with the sea.

13th Fife Reunion 1982. A gathering of past and present members and friends of the 13th Fife (Rosyth Methodist) held in the Church in October 1982 to mark the Group's fortieth anniversary.

2nd Fife Anniversary 1983. A photograph taken at the Glen Pavilion to mark the 2nd Fife
(YMCA) Scout Group seventy-fifth anniversary in December 1983.

Presentation of Tent to 49th Fife 1983. Captain Ian Powe of HMS Cochrane presents a new tent
to the 49th Fife (Rosyth). Among the leaders in the back row are Mary Kidd, John Sherwood,
Linda Sherwood, and David Thompson. In front of David is a young Andrew Holland.

Presentation of Colours to 83rd Fife 1986. Members of the 83rd Fife (Cairneyhill) with their recently dedicated Group colours. Leaders are Dougie Fotheringham on the left and Lindsay Morris on right. (Dunfermline Press).

48th Fife Beavers 1987. The St Bridget's Colony of the 48th Fife (Dalgety Bay) in 1987. Left to right back row: Elaine Pert; Donald Thornton; David Lund; Ian Wilson; Richard Sharp; Lesley Tennant; Krystyna Wasiak. Second back row: Andrew Haynes; -?-; David Forgen; Alan Tennant; -?-; David Lund. Second front row: Jean Reid; Richard Pert; Ewan Crozier; Andrew Craig; Graham Cross; Adrian Laurence; Kevin Nolan; Paul Morrison. Front row: -?-; Gerrard Consalvey; Darrel Mathers; Christopher Knight; Justin Andrews.

Presentations of Silver Acorns 1987. Three Scouters from Rosyth District who were presented with awards at the District AGM in April 1987 held in St Peter's Parish Church hall, Inverkeithing. John Lyson received the Bar to the Silver Acorn on stepping down after twenty years service as District Commissioner. Also retiring was Assistant District Commissioner Sarah Giles, 68th Fife (St Peter's Parish Church Inverkeithing), and she and Frank Pope, 13th Fife (Rosyth Methodist), received the Silver Acorn. The presentations were made by the Chief Commissioner for Scotland Garth Morrison (who was later appointed Chief Scout).

Presentations at 48th Fife 1989. Members of the 48th Fife (Dalgety Bay) receive awards at the Group's AGM in June 1987. Left to right back row: Jim Muir (Thanks Badge); Lynn Merckel and Peter Merckel (Leader Training Awards); David Hay and Colin Merckel (Chief Scout's Awards); DC Bob Liddle. Front row: Krystyna Wasiak and Anna Dodds (Leader Training Awards); Andrew Robertson, Barry O'Rourke and Graeme Cochrane (Chief Scout's Challenge) and Allan Dodds (Chief Scout's Award). (Dunfermline Press).

Presentation to Cyril McCord 1989. Members of the 62nd Fife (Crossford) look on as Area Commissioner Frank Hood presents the Medal of Merit to Group Scout Leader Cyril McCord in June 1989. (Dunfermline Press)

Bench in Memory of John Lyson 1990. On 27 May a bench (sited in the grounds of Rosyth Parish Church) was dedicated in memory of Rosyth District's former District Commissioner John Lyson who died in August 1989. Left to right standing: Gordon Stevenson; Frances Stephen; Alistair McGregor; Isobel McIlroy; Jean Shaw; Frank Hood; Jonathan Drever; Bill McIlroy; Bob Liddle; David Payne; Iain Smith; Phillip Parkyn; Tony Caudrey; Martin Rogers; John Henderson (?); Tony Bilton; Nicky Mathieson; Dot Wright; Hazel Connery; Milly Blyth. Sitting: Graham Bennett; Bill Webster; Sarah Giles; Jimmy Spence.

Presentations at 49th Fife 1990. The Chief Commissioner for Scotland, Dorothy Kinloch, presents Queen's Scout certificates to Debbie and Ian Symms of 49th Fife (Rosyth) Scout Group in December 1990.

Dunfermline District Cubs 1991. Cubs from Dunfermline District celebrated the Cub Section's seventy-fifth Anniversary with an It's a Knockout and party in the Glen in June. Daryl McKenzie of the 2nd Fife (YMCA) helps District Commissioner Ken Marshall to cut a celebration cake.

Presentation to Jim Tonner 1991. Jim Tonner of the 75th Fife (Carnock) is presented with an appointment as an Honorary Scouter on 'retiring' from Scouting. He is surrounded by members of the Group and in the back row (left to right) are Peter Adamson; District Commissioner Ken Marshall; Duncan Martin; Kirsten Moeller and Jean Martin. (Dunfermline Press).

New Colours for 61st Fife 1994. The 61st Fife (St John's RC Rosyth) were presented with new colours in April 1994. The adults are (left to right): Arthur Pain; Margaret Glancey; Derek Miller; David Dykes and Alan McCourt.

81st Fife Group 2000. A millennium photograph of the 81st Fife (1st Broomhall) outside their headquarters. This was taken following a Founder's Day service in February 2000. (Photo by Linsay Craig)

Rosyth District AGM 2001. Rosyth District's AGM was held in Rosyth Methodist Church in May 2001. Left to right in the front row are Area Commissioner Danny Barr, District Chairman Lee Symms, Chief Commissioner for Scotland Andy Matthews, Gordon Pert 48th Fife (Dalgety Bay), and District Commissioner Alan Bull.